Introduction

Maths & Sport — ages 9 to 11

This series of 'Maths and Topics' activity books is intended to bring to life the uses and importance of maths all around us. It achieves this by helping the children to apply their maths skills in contexts that are familiar and interesting to them. The books offer a variety of ways in which this can be achieved, while meeting the essential needs of the maths curriculum and national numeracy targets.

Each book deals with a particular topic. Each topic is, in turn, divided into five themes. These have been carefully designed and structured to develop the skills appropriate to the age and abilities of the children. The activities become progressively more complex and challenging; so each book has sufficient scope to encourage the less able and yet challenge the more able. The range and variety of these activities has been planned and set out with Primary mathematics curricula requirements, and national numeracy standards, very much to the fore.

Teachers' notes support each section of every book. These cover strategies for discussions, and suggestions for whole-class and individual exercises that introduce the concepts and the key maths vocabulary. Guidance is also offered on how to use and develop the activities within each theme. Many of the activities provide useful material for homework.

A record of achievement certificate is available at the end of each book to allow the children to record their progress.

Contents

Further information about Channel 4 Schools
programmes and
accompanying resources is
available from

Channel 4 Schools
PO Box 100
Warwick
CV34 6TZ

Tel: 01926 436 444
Fax: 01926 436 446

ISBN 1-86215-401-5

Written by Ian Bennett.
Edited by James Griffin and Liz Meenan.
Designed and produced by Crystal Presentations Ltd.
for Channel Four Learning Ltd.
Printed by Clarkeprint Ltd.

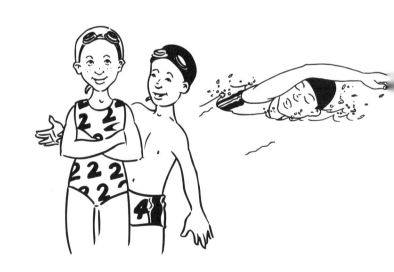

1.1 Swimming finals

Aims to encourage children to:
- read and interpret data tables and decimal fractions;
- sequence numbers to 1 decimal place;
- present data in alternative formats;
- recognise that data recording can provide information which informs decision making.

Discussion:
Talk about the uses of a stopwatch and get the children to draw their own conclusions about why we need more accurate measurements of time. Exercises relating to measurements of minutes and seconds can prepare pupils for a closer examination of fractions of a second.

Extension:
The classification of results from local and national sports events can researched by groups in the class using newspapers and internet.

1.2 Relay splash

Aims to encourage children to:
- improve their skills in addition, ordering and sequencing numbers to 2 decimal places;
- represent information graphically;
- interpret this representation to get further information.

Discussion:
Discuss the rules of relay races. It is important that children appreciate the range and variation of lap speeds in each team. Also include practice in the addition of decimal numbers and their application. Start with simple numbers as units of time to one decimal place. A number line exercise can help the children visualise the concept.

Extension:
Extend the exercise to 2 decimal places. Try rounding up and rounding down. Use actual results from different sporting events.

1.3 Running results

Aims to encourage children to:
- develop strategies for ordering numbers;
- classify and interpret data;
- use data to make decisions.

Discussion:
Beforehand, ask the children about various 'knock out' systems used in different sports. This applies to racing of all kinds. The exercise itself suits children working collaboratively in pairs. This will assist with double checking heats where 2 or more fast times are recorded.

Extension:
This classification and ordering exercise can be extended by providing data to two places of decimals. Other systems of finalist selections can be devised.

1.4 Relay results

Aims to encourage children to:
- read and classify to 2 places of decimals;
- make additions of decimal numbers;
- select and interpret data.

Discussion:
Pupils need to understand how relay races work. Revise decimal numbers ordering to 2 places. Use a results chart to help pupils to correctly identify the lane number and lap number.

Extension:
This exercise can be extended by getting the children to draw their own bar charts of the race. Discussion of suitable scales will be challenging.

1.5 Relay racing

Aims to encourage children to:
- read from ordered data tables;
- read and recognise number sequencing quickly and accurately from given data;
- practice addition of decimals.

Discussion:
This game develops the skills acquired from the previous 4 activity sheets. It can be visited regularly to improve practical numeracy and ordering skills in an enjoyable context. Some demonstration sequences will prove useful for weaker pupils.

Extension:
Resource sheet 1, page 33, will prove useful for 2 levels of difficulty for this exercise. Actual times from other sports and athletics events can also be used to provide additional variety and levels of challenge for children.

Swimming finals

Name

Here is the result of the 50m freestyle final.

	Lane 1	Lane 2	Lane 3	Lane 4	Lane 5	Lane 6
Swimmer	**Molly**	**Jane**	**Jasmin**	**Tracy**	**Leyla**	**Lara**
Time	**52.3sec**	**53.1sec**	**52.0sec**	**51.8sec**	**52.7sec**	**52.9sec**

➤ Look at the information above and complete the following sentences using the words **slowest**, **fastest**, **slower and faster**.

Tracy was the .... swimmer.

Jane was .... than Lara.

Leyla was .... than Molly, but .... than Jane.

➤ Complete the bar chart showing the race results.

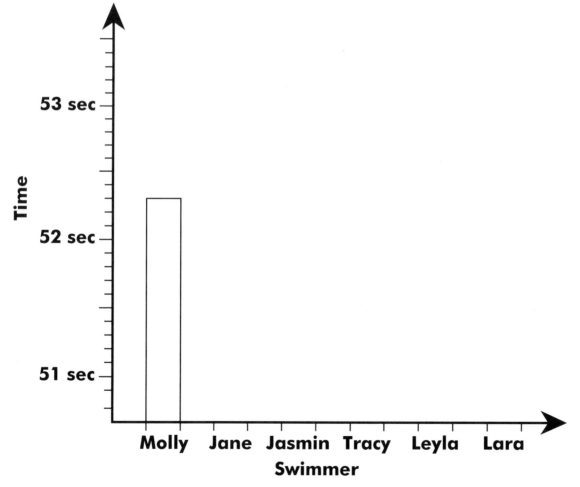

Challenge!

➤ Put the race results in order, starting with the fastest.

Relay splash

Name

The swimming relay final was exciting. Here are the results in seconds.

Swimmer	Lane 1	Lane 2	Lane 3	Lane 4	Lane 5	Lane 6
A	32.3	30.1	30.3	35.4	33.1	30.5
B	29.7	30.5	34.7	29.9	30.0	33.0
C	33.4	29.7	30.4	30.9	30.1	30.6
D	31.2	35.4	31.1	31.4	29.4	30.6
Total						

➤ Complete the bar chart below for each of the lanes.
Shade or colour in each lap differently.
Use the results to find out which lane won the race.

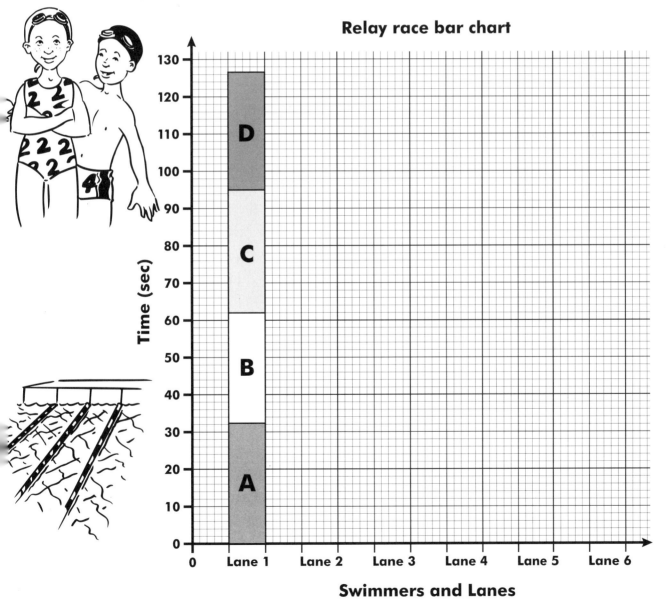

Relay race bar chart

➤ Lane .... won the race.

Running results

Name

A total of 36 girls entered the 100 metres race on Sports Day. There were 6 heats. Here are the results in seconds.

	Heat 1	Heat 2	Heat 3	Heat 4	Heat 5	Heat 6
Lane 1	18.4	17.9	19.0	20.7	21.3	22.4
Lane 2	20.1	22.1	20.2	21.6	22.7	20.1
Lane 3	22.5	20.2	17.8	18.0	23.4	21.2
Lane 4	18.3	24.1	21.3	24.6	20.1	23.4
Lane 5	19.1	18.4	22.1	18.3	22.1	19.7
Lane 6	21.2	22.0	18.7	23.2	21.6	18.6

➤ Write down the winner from each heat.

Heat 1	Lane	4	TIME	18.3 sec
Heat 2	Lane		TIME	
Heat 3	Lane		TIME	
Heat 4	Lane		TIME	
Heat 5	Lane		TIME	
Heat 6	Lane		TIME	

The heat winners will now run in a semi-final.

➤ Select another 6 runners for the 2nd semi-final.

Runner 1 Heat .... Lane ....   Runner 2 Heat .... Lane ....

Runner 3 Heat .... Lane ....   Runner 4 Heat .... Lane ....

Runner 5 Heat .... Lane ....   Runner 6 Heat .... Lane ....

➤ Are these the 12 fastest runners? ....

Challenge!

➤ Can you think of a better or fairer way for selecting the finalists?

Name

Five teams competed in the relay race. Each lap of the race was timed in seconds. Use the results table to answer the questions.

	Team 1	Team 2	Team 3	Team 4	Team 5
Lap 1	18.32	18.57	20.47	18.06	22.17
Lap 2	20.27	22.31	18.98	21.24	22.08
Lap 3	21.24	18.74	18.83	21.43	18.23
Lap 4	19.56	19.91	20.45	19.03	18.27
TOTAL	*79.39*				

➤ Work out the total time taken by each team, and complete the table.

➤ Which team won the relay race? ....

➤ Which team was ahead after lap 1?

   Team ....   Time ....seconds

➤ Which team was ahead after lap 2?

   Team ....   Time ....seconds

➤ Which team was ahead after lap 3?

   Team ....   Time ....seconds

The school is selecting a relay team for a local competition.

➤ Which 4 runners from any of the 5 teams would you select?

Team:	Lap number:	Time:
Team:	Lap number:	Time:
Team:	Lap number:	Time:
Team:	Lap number:	Time:

Challenge!

➤ Draw a bar chart of the race and use it to describe the race to a friend. Was it exciting? Was it a close finish?

Relay racing

Name

A game for 6 players.

You need: Resource Sheet 1 **Relay race times** (Table A), a dice and a calculator.

The aim of the game is to get the fastest relay racing team total.

How to play: Each player in turn throws the dice. If with the first throw the player scores a 4 then the first time is taken from **Lap 1, Lane 4**. If the next player with the first throw scores a 2 then their time is **Lap 1, Lane 2**. Players 3 to 6 follow the same procedure.

More than 1 player can have the same lap time. Laps 2, 3 and 4 follow the same procedure.

	Lap 1	Lap 2	Lap 3	Lap 4	Total
Player 1					
Player 2					
Player 3					
Player 4					
Player 5					
Player 6					

At the end of lap 4 the players total their lap times and the winner is the player with the lowest total time.

➤ Play the game again, but this time use Table B from Resource Sheet 1.

2.1 Sporting symmetry

Aims to encourage children to:
• develop skills in recognising lines of reflective symmetry and their applications.

Discussion:
Sports grounds and pitches are ideal starting points for real-life applications of symmetry. School gyms and sports grounds can provide useful examples to view and examine.

Asymmetrical designs such as the rounders pitch gives an example where both teams are not engaged in the same activity simultaneously. Squared paper for the Challenge is provided on Resource Sheet 2.

Extension:
Scale drawings of various school sporting layouts can be developed using only limited measurements and symmetry.

2.2 Football fractions

Aims to encourage children to:
• use symmetry in a practical way;
• apply knowledge of simple fractions;
• recognise regular shapes and their names.

Discussion:
Class work can introduce simple examples of reflection and rotation to make simple shapes and patterns. Cutting out shapes and

reflections will assist the children to visualise the possibilities available.

Extension:
A variant for children would be the development of a sequence of reflection/rotation/reflection to achieve the same end - the creation of the football pitch design - other sports pitches could be attempted using layouts from the previous exercise.

2.3 Netball plan

Aims to encourage children to:
• practise measurement, scale drawing and area calculations.

Discussion:
Children could be encouraged to talk about size and areas and perimeters of different sporting facilities. Tasks can can be related to a suitable playing pitch. Some preparation work on calculations will be essential, e.g. the 3 x 3 metres square calculation used in

the 1cm representing 3 metres. Drawing this to a larger scale and dividing the 1m squares to show the 3 x 3 build up to the $9m^2$ will be helpful. Squared paper for the Challenge is provided on Resource Sheet 2.

Extension:
Strategies to work on irregular shapes and their areas can be introduced. Work on the area of circles and semi-circles could also be developed.

2.4 Sporting shapes

Aims to encourage children to:
• develop skills in recognising standard mathematical shapes in common use;
• develop strategies for classifying shapes.

Discussion:
Classwork could begin with a review of the

common figures found in sporting venues. A review of circles, semi-circles, quadrants, squares, ovals, sectors of circles would be useful preparation for the activity.

Extension:
Some work will be needed showing embedded shapes within shapes, e.g. the rectangles within the tennis court and football pitch.

2.5 Team spirit

Aims to encourage children to:
• practise using co-ordinates;
• develop strategies for using number combinations;
• reinforce numeracy skills with simple addition and subtraction.

Discussion:
Children will need practice in adding and subtracting (x,y) values to move from one

co-ordinate to another. Decisions on which values to use for each dice thrown must be explained using examples.

Extension:
'Teamwork' can be encouraged with one partner checking combinations while the other checks on routes to goal.

Sporting symmetry

Name

You need: A mirror and a ruler.
Here is half of a hockey pitch.

60m

16m

25m   25m

Scale: 1cm
represents 10m

➤ Use a mirror to see the other half of the hockey pitch.

➤ Draw the lines of reflective symmetry. How many lines of
symmetry has the hockey pitch got altogether?

Here are other sports pitches.

➤ Investigate the number of lines of symmetry each pitch has and
draw them.

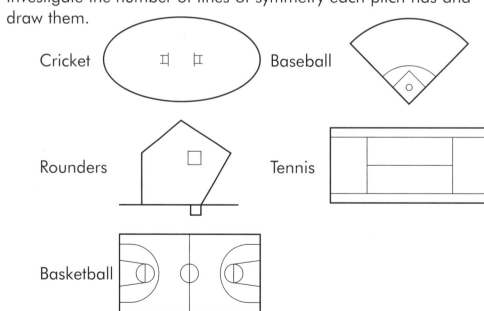

Cricket   Baseball

Rounders   Tennis

Basketball

Challenge!

➤ Draw the hockey pitch to scale on squared paper.

Football fractions

You need: A mirror, a ruler and a compass.

Here is part of a football pitch.

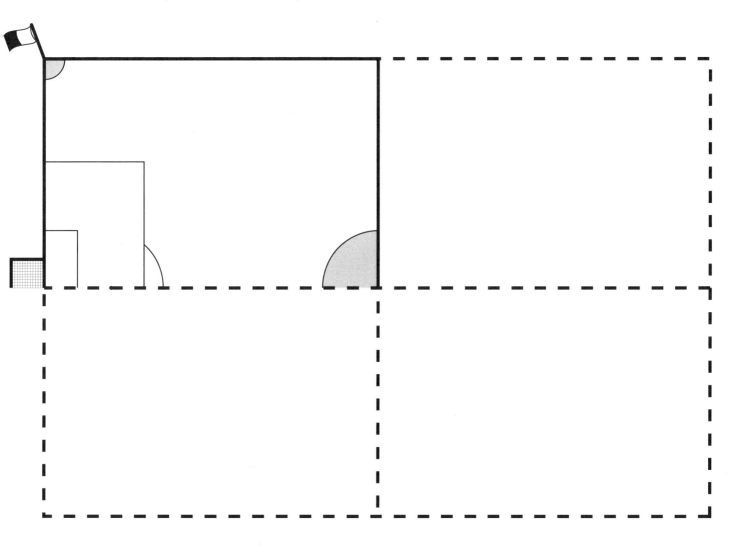

➤ What fraction of the pitch is given? ....

➤ What fraction of the pitch is missing? ....

➤ Complete the pitch by using the 2 lines of symmetry.

➤ How many rectangles can you find?

➤ How many circles can you see?

➤ Shade the 4 quadrants of a circle. 1 is shaded for you.

➤ Colour the areas which are segments of a circle.

Netball plan

Name

Yasmin's school is planning a new netball pitch. Here is the scale drawing they have made.

Scale: 1cm represents 2 m

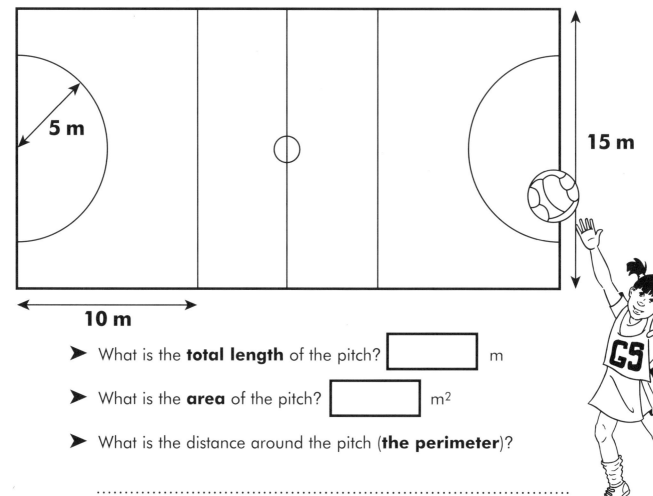

➤ What is the **total length** of the pitch? ☐ m

➤ What is the **area** of the pitch? ☐ m²

➤ What is the distance around the pitch (**the perimeter**)?

....

The pitch is made up from 3 **equal rectangles**.

➤ Find and colour the rectangles using 3 different colours.

➤ What **fraction** of the pitch's area is each rectangle? ☐

Challenge!

➤ Draw the netball pitch on squared paper using the **scale:** 1cm represents 1 metre. How many rectangles can you find **altogether** on the netball pitch. Compare your answer with a partner. Estimate the area of the semi-circles by counting the squares. Estimate what fraction of the pitches area is covered by the semi-circles.

Sporting shapes

Name

These sports pitches use lots of shapes. Match each pitch to its description.

Baseball

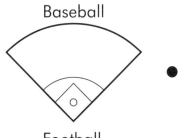

●   ● | only rectangles!

Football

●   ● | 1 pentagon,
2 squares,
1 straight line

Rounders

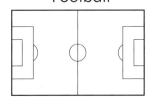

●   ● | 3 equal rectangles,
2 semi-circles,
1 circle

Tennis

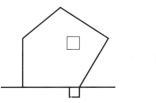

●   ● | 1 oval,
4 pairs of
parallel lines

Cricket

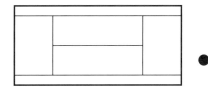

●   ● | 6 rectangles
1 circle,
2 sectors of a circle

Netball

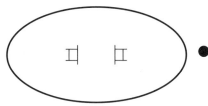

●   ● | 1 large quadrant,
1 small quadrant,
1 square, 1 circle

Challenge!

➤ Describe the shapes in your favourite playing pitch.

Team spirit

Name

A game for 2 players

You need: 2 dice and a 'football' disk marker, and Resource Sheet 3, **Board game**.

Rules - Amateur level (single dice throws only)

Decide who plays at home and who plays away. The Home player starts and plays towards the goal mouth at (7, 3). Throw the dice and 'kick' the ball to the point on the dice score e.g. dice score 6 and 5 the ball lands on (6, 5) or, if the player prefers, (5, 6).

The **home player** can **add 1** to the **x number** to score, e.g. (6, 3) dice score becomes (7, 3) - GOAL. (7, 2), (7, 3), (7, 4) count as goals.

The **away player** can **subtract 1** from the **x number** to score, e.g. (2, 3) becomes (1, 3) - GOAL. (1, 2), (1, 3), (1, 4) count as goals.

The winner is the first to score 3 goals.

Rules - Professional level (adding and subtracting dice scores)

Play starts with the 'ball' in the centre of the football field (4, 3). Each dice score is used to 'kick' the ball forwards or backwards towards the opponent's goal.

Thus '3' and '1' moves the player's ball 3 steps along the x axis (backwards **or** forwards) and 1 step up or down the y axis or if the player prefers (1, 3) move 1 step along the x axis and 3 steps up **or** down the y axis.

The home player scores a goal by landing on or going past co-ordinate (7, 3) or (8, 3).

The away player scores a goal by landing on or going past co-ordinate (1, 3) or (0, 3).

The away player must **subtract** his/her **x** score to get back to the home goal. Both players can add or subtract the second dice score to move up or down the field (the y number).

When a goal is scored play restarts on (4, 3). If the ball moves off the pitch when it has been 'kicked', play continues from the point on the touchline where the ball left the pitch.

The first team to score 2 goals wins the game.

3.1 Sporting choices 1

Aims to encourage children to:
- read and interpret Venn diagrams;
- develop logical thinking;
- apply their conclusions in realistic contexts.

Discussion:
This work can be introduced by relating it to the class's own favourite sports. Simple examples of 'James likes football and cricket' shows James' position in the set, 'Naomi likes football but not cricket' - again

clearly showing the correct location, can give practice in placing choices in the correct segment of the sets.

All the logical 'and' and 'only' locations need to be understood before attempting this exercise.

Extension:
This can be developed to exercises where some examples are outside the set choices i.e. somebody who likes neither football, netball, nor swimming.

3.2 Sporting choices 2

Aims to encourage children to:
- present data in Venn diagram format;
- read and apply statements accurately;
- develop logical thinking.

Discussion:
Develop key questions to guide children into placing answers into their correct categories. Example could begin with simple 3 choice situations 'likes cricket; likes tennis; likes

cricket and tennis'. This can then progress to choice situations. Likes cricket but not tennis, etc. until a range of 8 options are available.

Extension:
The challenge offers the opportunity to pose problems where children have to deduce 1 or more of the missing subsets e.g. all 14 like cricket, 6 like cricket and basketball only, 4 like tennis only, 2 like all 3 sports. How many like cricket only?

3.3 Sailing the course

Aims to encourage children to:
- practise in marking bearings and applying them in real-life contexts.

Discussion:
Practice in the use of the protractor is important for this exercise. Children must also be made aware that the orientation of

North may not always be upright on the page. Discussion of how ships, boats and planes navigate will help to put this exercise into a meaningful perspective.

Extension:
A game to get to Treasure Island can link the use of angle bearings with co-ordinates. This can help towards understanding applications of latitude and longitude.

3.4 Time trials

Aims to encourage children to:
- interpret data presented in graphical format;
- deduce additional facts from the graph.

Discussion:
The class will have to practise choosing which units of measurement and scales to use for various distance/time graphs. The unit of distance can be varied, e.g. miles,

kilometres or laps, with the time unit being varied from hours or minutes. Ask questions such as 'How much time was passed from the start when the car is at this point?' (15 minutes) 'How much time has passed altogether when the car has reached the finish?'

Extension:
This exercise can be applied to children's own sporting and leisure activities such as laps of a track, outings and holiday trips.

3.5 Yacht race

Aims to encourage children to:
- devise a suitable scale for line graphs;
- deduce facts from a graph which they have made.

Discussion:
This will need to centre around suitable units of time and distance. Some

explanation may be needed for the nautical miles unit of measurement.

Extension:
Children can create distance/time graphs for a wide variety of sporting activities carried out in school. These can be based on actual measurements of distance and time which have been recorded by the class itself.

Sporting choices 1

Name

Here is a Venn diagram showing some children's favourite sporting choices.

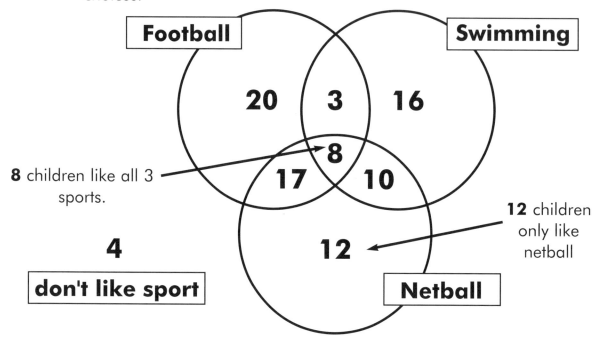

Football 20 3 16 **Swimming**

8 children like all 3 sports.

8

17 8 10

4 12

12 children only like netball

don't like sport **Netball**

➤ Use the Venn diagram to complete these answers.

12	only like netball
	only like swimming
	only like football
	like both football and swimming
	like both football and netball
	like both netball and swimming
8	like all three sports.

➤ There were .... children in the survey.

Challenge!

➤ How many children altogether like only 1 sport?

➤ How many children altogether like only 2 sports?

Name	

A group of 33 children were asked about their choices of 3 sports. Here are their answers.

like tennis only	2
like cricket only	3
like basketball only	5
like both tennis and cricket	6
like both basketball and tennis	4
like both cricket and basketball	3

The remaining children like all 3 sports.

➤ How many like all 3 sports? ☐

➤ Complete the Venn diagram to show the results.

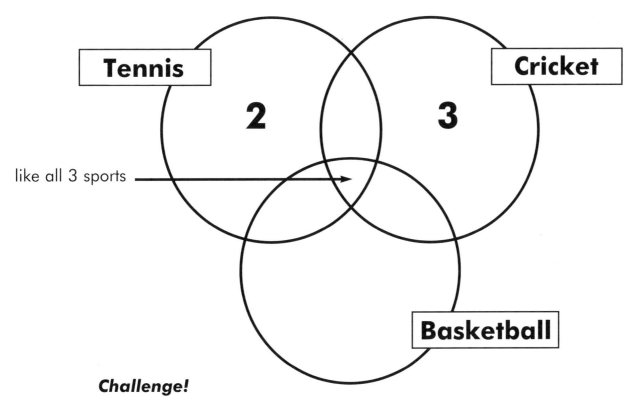

Challenge!

➤ Choose 3 sports and conduct a survey of your own class. Show your results on a Venn diagram.

Sailing the course

Name

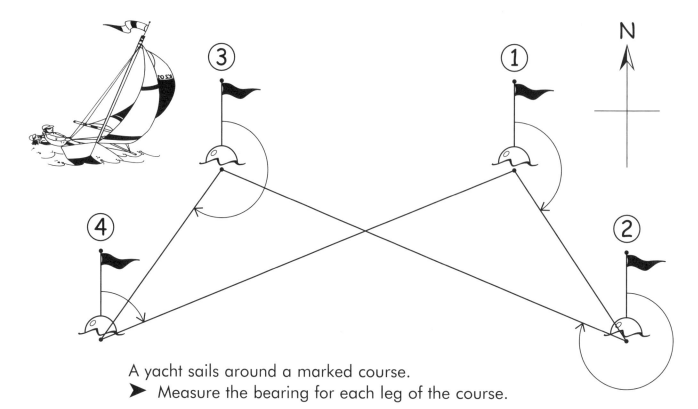

A yacht sails around a marked course.
➤ Measure the bearing for each leg of the course.

Buoy 1 to Buoy 2	Bearing ....145°..........
Buoy 2 to Buoy 3	Bearing ....
Buoy 3 to Buoy 4	Bearing ....
Buoy 4 to Buoy 1	Bearing ....

What if the yacht were to sail the course in opposite direction?

➤ Measure the bearings for each leg of this new course.

Buoy 1 to Buoy 4	Bearing ....
Buoy 4 to Buoy 3	Bearing ....
Buoy 3 to Buoy 2	Bearing ....
Buoy 2 to Buoy 1	Bearing ....

Challenge!

➤ Use the first set of answers to find the last set of answers
without using a protractor. Explain how you can do it.

Time trials

Name

Paul and Jason watched a motor race time trial. They used a stop watch to time each lap and each stop for 1 car. Afterwards they made this graph.

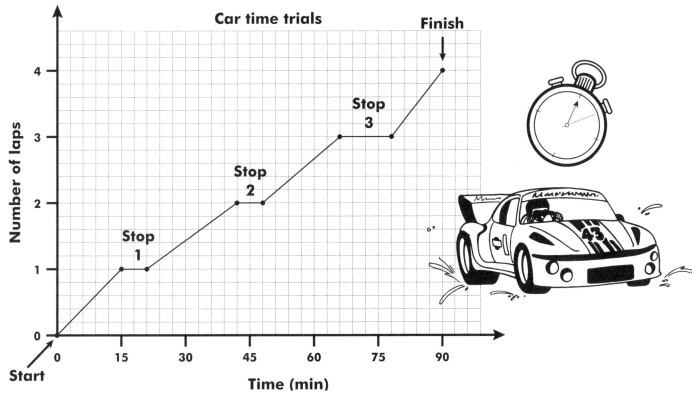

Car time trials

Use the graph to answer these questions.

➤ Altogether, the car travelled [   ] laps.

➤ Each lap is 5 kilometres, so how far did the car travel altogether? [   ] km

➤ How long altogether did the car spend moving? [   ] min

➤ The driver stopped after each lap to have his tyres checked. How many minutes did he stop for after:

the first lap? [   ] min

the second lap? [   ] min

the third lap? [   ] min

➤ How long did the first lap take to complete? [   ] min

➤ How long did the fourth lap take to complete? [   ] min

Yacht race

Name

A sailing course is 12 nautical miles long. It takes yacht **A** 60 mins to sail the course.

➤ What is its average speed in nautical miles per hour?

Yacht **B** takes 30 minutes more than yacht **A** to sail the course.

➤ What is its average speed in nautical miles per hour?

➤ Draw the line graph for yacht **B**. The line for yacht **A** is shown.

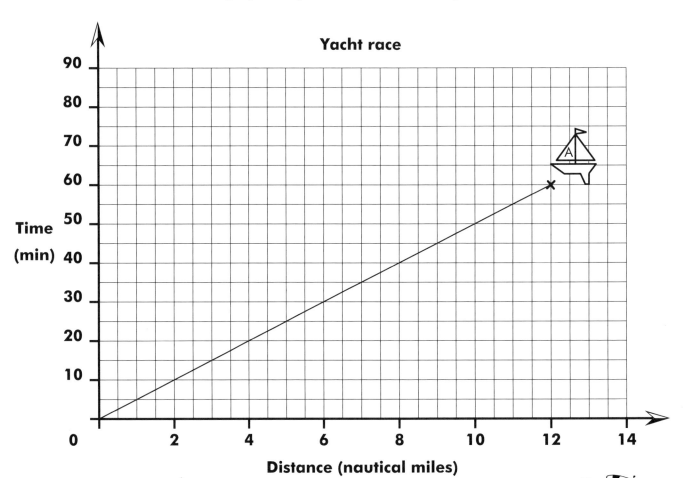

Yacht race

Time (min) — vertical axis: 10, 20, 30, 40, 50, 60, 70, 80, 90

Distance (nautical miles) — horizontal axis: 0, 2, 4, 6, 8, 10, 12, 14

➤ Use the graph to help you to estimate how far ahead yacht **A** is:

after 30 minutes ....

after 45 minutes ....

when yacht A finishes ....

Challenge!

➤ Another yacht **C** wins the race by 5 minutes. Draw yacht **C**'s line graph. Calculate how far ahead of yacht **A** the yacht **C** is when it finishes the race.

Maths & Sport © 1998 Channel Four Learning Ltd.

4.1 Home and away

Aims to encourage children to:
- explore number patterns;
- to tabulate results.

Discussion:
The topic can be introduced by discussing competitions and leagues entered into by the school in various sports. Ask questions such as 'How many games are played?'; 'Where are they played?'; 'How many teams are involved?' When children are familiar with playing combinations for small groups - say 3 teams, introduce the exercise.

Extension:
Ask the children to find other examples of local football, tennis, etc, and make up diagrams for these fixtures. Children then explain how the diagrams are planned.

4.2 Routes to goal

Aims to encourage children to:
- practise multiple arithmetic operations quickly and accurately.

Discussion:
Football passing involves speed and accuracy. The class can be reminded that the numeracy skills here require similar attention and accuracy. Classwork can begin by showing the class how the first correct route works. Also explain how they can move diagonally and downwards.

Extension:
Resource Sheet 2 can be photocopied and the operations and numbers modified to offer the children additional variety and challenge. To make it more challenging additional moves to the left, right and diagonally can also be introduced.

4.3 Shooting angles

Aims to encourage children to:
- measure angles accurately and apply angle measurements in a relevant context.

Discussion:
Introduce a range of angles of varying sizes in classroom and playground contexts, e.g. the angle range available by opening a door. Rolling a ball through the door with it opened at varying degrees up to 90° can help to illustrate the applications of this exercise.

Extension:
Starting from the 'penalty spot' ask the children to draw examples of obtuse, right and acute angles and say what the practical implications are of these angle sizes for kicking and scoring.

4.4 League scores

Aims to encourage children to:
- solve simple problems using combinations of multiplication and addition;
- use logical mathematical thinking to solve problems of missing number information.

Discussion:
Classwork should revise the logical problems related to using 3 additions to make the total 10. This should then be linked to the key multiplication values associated with football league scoring systems.

Extension:
The numeracy exercises related to this type of scoring table are linked to a logical constraint: that only 1 team can win all its games if it plays all the other teams, with the next highest scoring team having to lose at least 1 match. Many exercises can be developed from extending the number of teams and, hence, the number of games.

4.5 Passing angles

Aims to encourage children to:
- extend their practice of angle measurement;
- practise changes of direction and using and applying terms like 'clockwise' and 'anticlockwise'.

Discussion:
Discuss and practise clockwise and anticlockwise movements and changes of direction in classroom or playground. Start with right angles and angles of 45°. When these are grasped introduce a range of angle measurements - the direction of rotation clockwise and anticlockwise can be added.

Extension:
Get pupils to reverse the angle of turn - clockwise to anticlockwise, etc. Pupils can practise writing instructions to get from goal to goal - adding distance to movement instructions, e.g. 60° clockwise from the goal line, forward 6m, 70° anticlockwise, 8m forward.

Home and away

Name

In a particular league there are 4 teams - the All Stars, the Bright Sparks, the Bouncing Bears and the Terrible Tigers.

Each team plays the other 3 teams twice in a season, once at home, once away.

A record is kept of all the games played by all the teams in this chart.

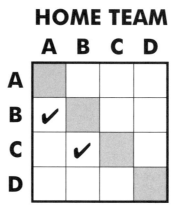

HOME TEAM

	A	**B**	**C**	**D**
A	▨			
B	✔	▨		
C		✔	▨	
D				▨

AWAY TEAM

3 games have been played so far, team A has played team B at home. Team B has played team C at home.

➤ Which other game has been played?

Team [　] played team [　] ....

➤ How many games will be played altogether in the season?

➤ Why are some boxes in the chart shaded?

....

....

➤ If the league expands to 5 teams, draw a home and away chart on the back of this sheet for this bigger league.

➤ How many games will each team play altogether in this new league?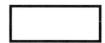

Challenge!

➤ Investigate the number of games played by 6, 7 and 8 teams and so on. Explain your results.

Name

Your teacher will tell you how to play the game.

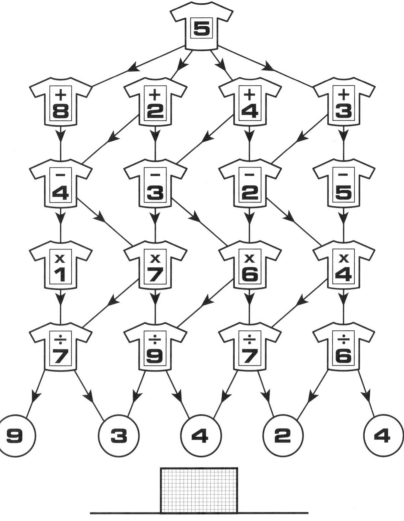

➤ Find as many correct routes to goal as possible.
➤ Mark each one in a different colour.

Route		+	−	x	÷	Goal
1	5	8	4	7	7	9
2	5	3	2			
3	5	2				
4	5					
5	5					

Challenge!

➤ Use Resource Sheet 2 to make up other routes to goal.

Shooting angles

Name

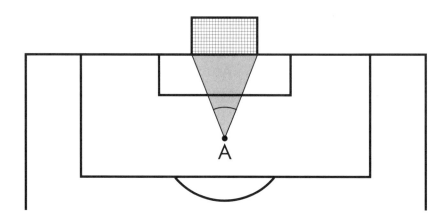

You need: A protractor.

Player A is taking a penalty kick. To score he must keep his shot inside the shaded triangle.

➤ Use a protractor to measure the shooting angle at A. ◻ °

➤ Here are 5 other players kicking for goal. Measure their shooting angles and record the answers in the table below.

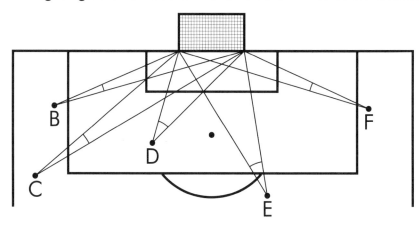

Player	B	C	D	E	F
Shooting angle (°)					

➤ Who do you estimate has the best shooting angle?

Player ◻

Challenge!

➤ Compare your answer with a partner and explain your reason.

League scores

Name

Here are this year's football league results.

In this league the points are awarded as follows.

Win 3 points, **Draw** 1 point, **Lose** 0 points

➤ Work out the missing results from the table below.

	Played	Won	Drawn	Lost	Total
Athletico	10	5	4	1	19
Belton Blues	10	5		3	17
Dyno Drivers	10	3			16
Partico	10		2		11
Chelton	10		3		9
Winfield	10		6	4	

➤ What is the maximum points any team can be awarded in a season?

➤ What must a team do to get maximum points?

A team must .... all their games at home and away.

➤ How many teams can win maximum points?

Explain ....

....

➤ What is the least number of points a team can get?

➤ How many teams can get this number of points?

Challenge!

➤ If one team gets maximum points, what is the next highest possible score another team can get?

Passing angles

Name

You need: a circular protractor and a ruler.
Here is the passing plan used by the school team to score a goal.

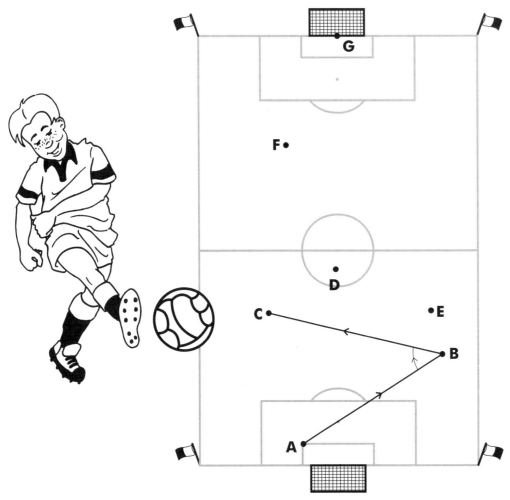

The path of the ball for the first 2 passes has been drawn,
(player **A** passes to player **B** then **B** to **C**). **B** turns 45° clockwise
and passes to **C**.

➤ Draw in the lines to show the path of the ball from **C** to **D**,
D to **E**, **E** to **F** and **F** to **G**.

➤ Measure the angle of turn made by the player at each point
and write whether the angle is acute, obtuse or reflex.

➤ Write the direction of turn for each player.

player **B** turned	45°°	Acute	Clockwise
player **C** turned	..............°	....	Anti-clockwise
player **D** turned	..............°	....	....
player **E** turned	..............°	....	....
player **F** turned	..............°	....	....

5.1 Medal madness

Aims to encourage children to:
• practise making reasonable estimates in relating units of measure correctly to appropriate activities.

Discussion:
Introduce various sporting activities which have units of length as their distinguishing

feature - long jump, high jump, etc. Discuss the range and variety of these units of length which are do not depend on the time it takes the competitor to carry them out. Use examples of activities where distance related to time inferences need to be applied.

Extension:
Use other track and field events to make estimates and calculations of appropriate units of distance and time.

5.2 Away games

Aims to encourage children to:
• practise marking co-ordinates and reading and following diagrammatic instructions.

Discussion:
This exercise can be introduced by discussing with the children about the use of co-ordinates to locate position. 'How far right/left (x)?', 'How far up/down (y)?'.

Move to combining two x y co-ordinate movements in sequence before undertaking the exercise.

Extension:
Children practise checking co-ordinate directions for themselves, with some examples being invalid. The children then could highlight the problem co-ordinate.

5.3 Team fractions

Aims to encourage children to:
• practise applying percentage calculations;
• relate fractions and percentages in a visual format;
• apply percentages to different quantities.

Discussion:
Revise class understanding of percentages with suitable examples. For example ask about class attendance at various activities -

100%, 50%, etc. and relate these to the correct fractions of the class.

Extension:
The new coach activity relates the exercise to a new 100% context. This can be a starting point for similar percentage exercises relating to other units of measurement such as distance, time and volume.

5.4 Bull's-eye

Aims to encourage children to:
• practise multiplication, calculation of averages and data presentation.

Discussion:
The activity can be developed around an archery scoring system (10 rings - scoring 0 to 10). Calculations can begin with scoring combinations from 'maximum score' to

'minimum score' (360 to 0) if you miss. The scores between 0 and 360 can then be discussed, leading on to finding a mean (average) score rather than an 'actual' one.

Extension:
A pie chart presentation of data can be developed for this exercise and other applications, including the examples from activity 5.3.

5.5 Olympic time

Aims to encourage children to:
• calculate additions and subtractions of time units;
• make deductions related to world time zones.

Discussion:
The class should be introduced to the world time zones starting with Greenwich Mean Time and working towards the East (+) and

West (-). Revise the children's understanding of another place in the world being 12 hours behind/ahead of Greenwich.

Extension:
Work on time and longitude units to show the relationship between 180° E and 180° W and the 24 hour clock. The 360 degrees in a circle can be related to the 24 hour clock.

Medal madness

Name

➤ Match the medal to the world record holder.

Challenge!

➤ Make up a set of medals for 6 other sporting records which either require distance or time measurements.

Name

The Olympic bus takes the athletes to different venues. The bus can only travel **up**, **down** or **across** the **one-way** streets as shown.

If the bus starts from the Olympic village and travels to the Cycle stadium at (3, 2), its route is (0, 0), (0, 1), (0, 2), (1, 2), (2, 2) and (3, 2).

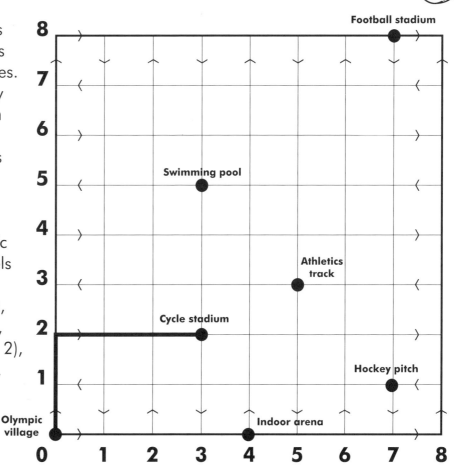

➤ Draw the one-way route and write out the co-ordinates for the following bus routes. Some routes have been started for you.

Cycle stadium to Swimming pool (3, 2), (4, 2), (4, 3),
....

Swimming pool to Athletics track (3, 5), (3, 4), (4, 4),
....

Athletics track to Football stadium (5, 3), (4, 3),
....

Football stadium to Hockey pitch
....

Hockey pitch to Indoor arena
....

Challenge!

➤ Select and draw a route which visits all the places on the map starting at the village. Write out the co-ordinates for the route.

Team fractions

Name

The Olympic coach holds 20 people. If it has 20 people on board it is said to be 100% full.

➤ Calculate what percentage of the coach is filled when each of the following teams travel to competitions. Shade in the coach to help you work out the answers.

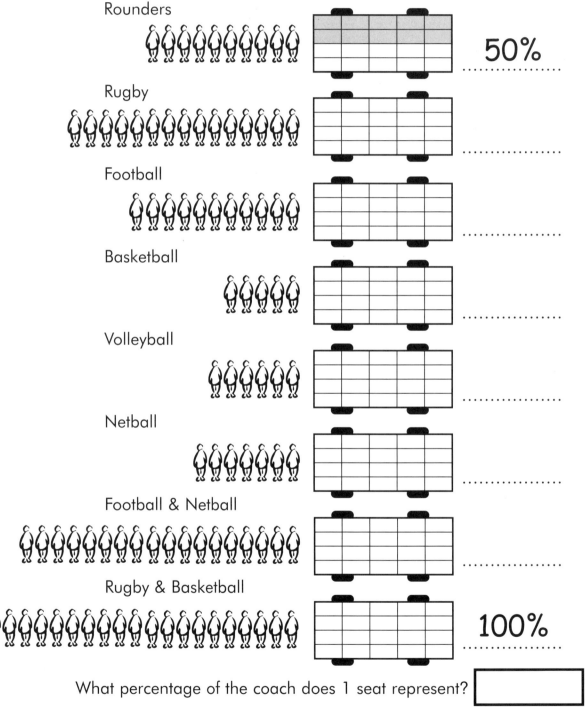

Rounders

50% ....

Rugby

....

Football

....

Basketball

....

Volleyball

....

Netball

....

Football & Netball

....

Rugby & Basketball

100% ....

What percentage of the coach does 1 seat represent?

Challenge!

➤ If another bus has 30 seats, calculate what the percentage of this coach the teams would occupy on the way to the events.

Activity 5.3 | **Maths & Sport** | © 1998 Channel Four Learning Ltd.

Bull's-eye

Name

Each player starts with 36 arrows.
The 'bull's-eye' score per arrow is 10.

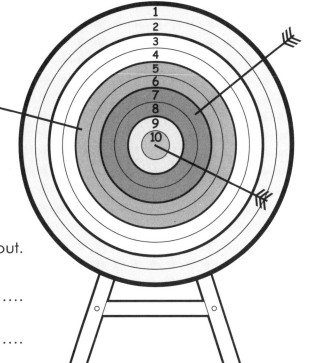

➤ What is the maximum possible
   score? ....

One archer scored 340 points after
36 arrows. Her average score per arrow
was 9.4.

➤ Explain how this answer was worked out.

   ....

   ....

   ....

➤ Now find the average score per arrow for each of these results.
   Give your answers to the nearest whole number.

Average score
per arrow

....

Average score
per arrow

....

Average score
per arrow

....

Challenge!

➤ Think of an easy way to show each final score as a
   piechart.

Olympic time

Name

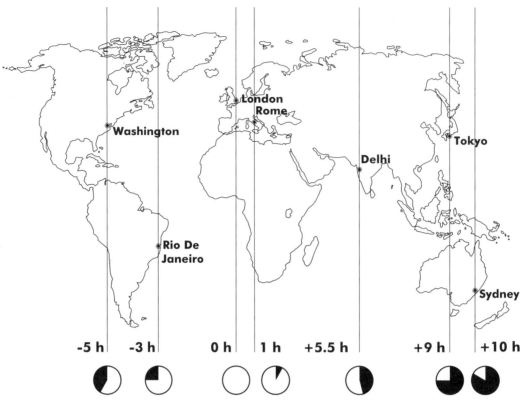

-5 h   **-3 h**   **0 h**   **1 h**   **+5.5 h**   **+9 h**   **+10 h**

➤ On the map above are marked the time differences between some cities. If the Olympic games are held in Rome calculate the actual time in each country for the final day's events. Some have been done for you.

Events & times in Rome		Washington	Rio	London	Delhi	Tokyo	Sydney
Javelin	9.30am			8.30am			
100m Running	11.00am				4.30pm		
200m Freestyle	11.30am						
Discus	12.15pm						
High Jump	12.25pm						
800m Running	1.00pm		9.00am				
Pole Vault	1.05pm						
Triple Jump	2.25pm						
400m Running	3.08pm						
400m Relay	3.22pm						

Challenge!

➤ On the back of this sheet calculate a revised timetable if the Olympics took place in Tokyo.

Resource sheet 1 - Relay race times

All times are given in seconds.

TABLE A

	Lap 1	Lap 2	Lap 3	Lap 4
Lane 1	32.3	29.7	33.4	31.2
Lane 2	30.1	30.5	29.7	35.4
Lane 3	30.3	34.7	30.4	31.1
Lane 4	35.4	29.9	30.9	31.4
Lane 5	33.1	30.0	30.1	29.4
Lane 6	30.5	33.0	30.6	30.6

TABLE B

	Lap 1	Lap 2	Lap 3	Lap 4
Lane 1	32.32	29.68	33.44	31.15
Lane 2	30.09	30.47	29.65	35.40
Lane 3	30.34	34.72	30.39	31.06
Lane 4	35.36	29.91	30.94	31.44
Lane 5	33.11	29.96	30.06	29.38
Lane 6	30.54	33.01	30.55	30.60

Resource sheet 2 - Routes to goal

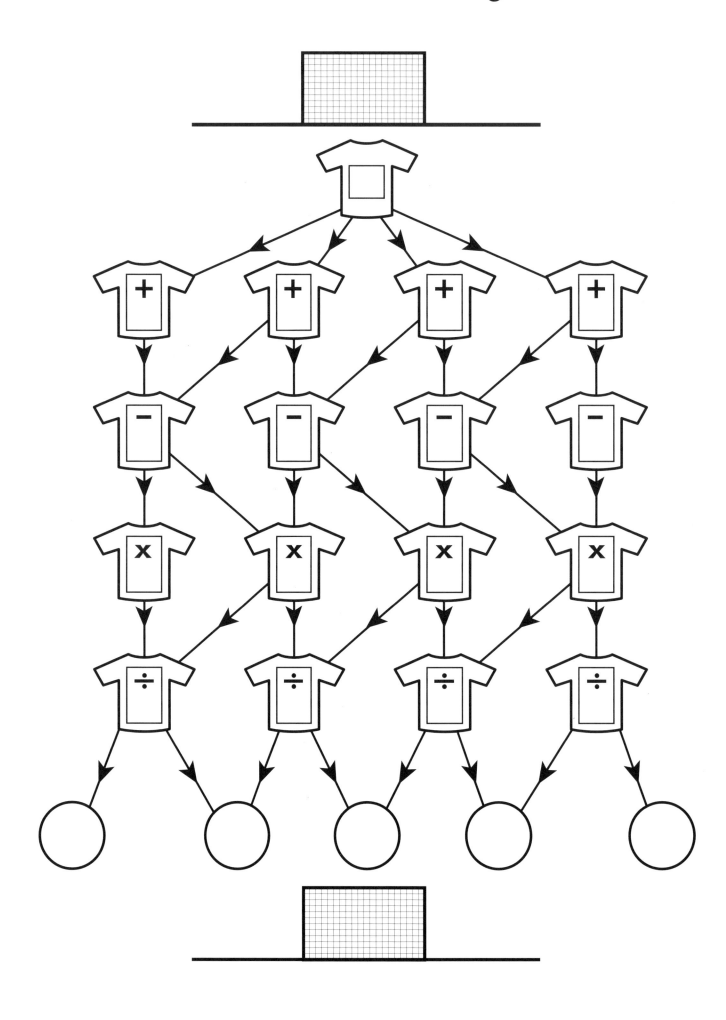

Resource 2 **Maths & Sport** © 1998 Channel Four Learning Ltd.

Resource sheet 3 - Game board

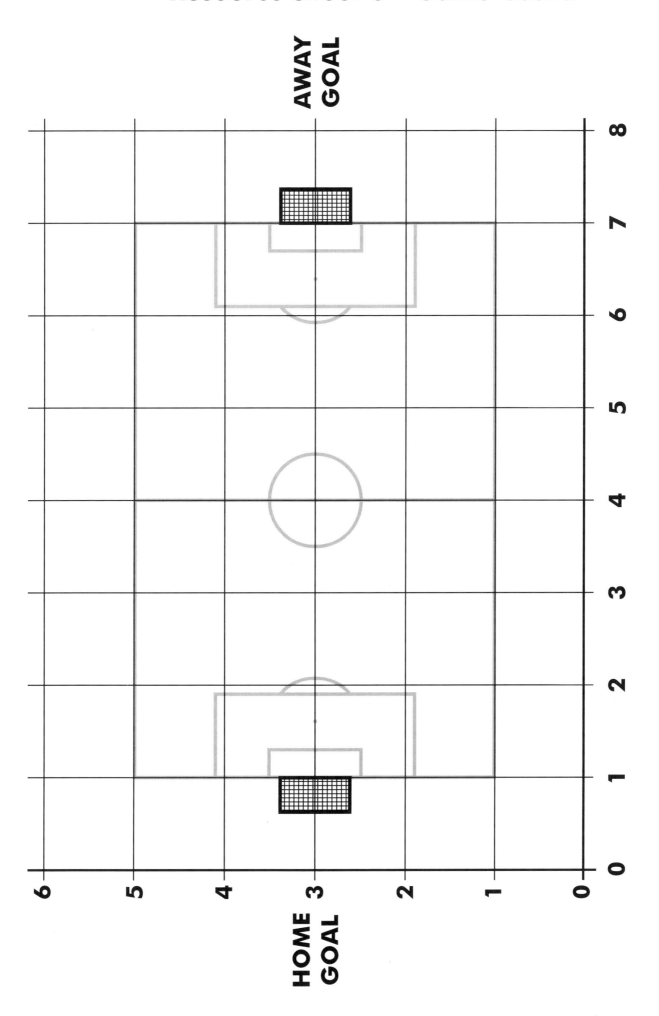

AWAY GOAL

HOME GOAL

Maths & Sport

Record of Achievement

Name _____ **Date** _____

My favourite activity was _____

I liked it because _____

_____

I found some activities difficult, such as _____

_____

because _____

_____

_____

I have learnt how to _____

_____

_____

I would like to have more practice with _____

_____

_____

_____